Cryptocurrency trading

A beginner guide to understand blockchain world and effective strategies to trading crypto and make profit

Anthony Satoshi

Copyright 2021 © Anthony Satoshi
All right reserved
ISBN

Table of Contents

Table of Contents 3
Introduction 6
Chapter 1: It All Starts with a Block 8
   Theoretical start 10
   Blockchain components 12
Chapter 2: Understanding Cryptocurrency 16
   Pricing 17
   Cryptocurrencies to watch 23
Chapter 3: Cryptocurrency Trading ... 26
   Making a good trade 30
   Picking an exchange 31
   Exchanges to keep in mind 35
   Initial offerings 36
   Tips for success 39
   Keep an eye on Ethereum 42
   5 Trading Mistakes to Avoid 45
Chapter 4: Mining 49
   Get into the mining game 50
Chapter 5: Creating a Personalized Trading Plan 59
   Consider trading goals 59

Consider your risk tolerance 60
Consider trading limits.............................. 61
Consider your ideal level of involvement .. 61
Consider your familiarity with trading..... 62
Consider your strengths and weaknesses .63
Consider the other challenges in your life at the moment..63
Stick with it 64
Don't be too anxious to get started............65

Chapter 6: Trading Strategies to Try .. 67
Long Position 67
Short Position Trading 67
Trading Analysis 68
Bullish and Bearish Markets 69
Volume 70
Charts 71
Candlesticks 71
Resistance and Support............................. 83
Considerations.. 85
Risk Management..................................... 85
Risk and Reward....................................... 86
Scaling Out into Parabolic Moves 87
Size Positions Appropriately 88

Chapter 7: The Future of Cryptocurrencies 89
    Capital markets 89
    Banking 90
    Digital Transactions 91
    Real Estate 93
    Public services 94
    Industry 96
Conclusion 98

Introduction

Congratulations on downloading *Cryptocurrency trading: A beginner guide to understand blockchain world and effective strategies to trading crypto and make profit* and thank you for doing so. The cryptocurrency explosion that has taken place over the past 10 years could have never been predicted, largely because cryptocurrency as a whole is an entirely new concept. While many people have already made millions off the growth to this point, the good news is there is still plenty of time to take advantage of this once in a lifetime opportunity.

To give you all the tools you need to do so, the following chapters will discuss everything you need to get started with cryptocurrency effectively, starting with a complete overview of the basics of cryptocurrency, what its used for and why people are so caught up with it these days. Next you will learn everything you need to know about the reigning king of cryptocurrencies, Bitcoin, and how to get involved with them today.

From there you will learn all about investing in Bitcoin and how to apply the buy and hold strategy to see returns that more traditional investors would kill for. You will then learn how to make yourself a part of the system, while still making a profit by mining bitcoins. Finally, you will learn about how world powers are poised to change cryptocurrency forever when you learn about the future of cryptocurrency.

There are plenty of books on this subject on the market, thanks again for choosing this one! Every effort was made to ensure it is full of as much useful information as possible, please enjoy!

Chapter 1: It All Starts with a Block

By this point it is unlikely that you haven't heard the term cryptocurrency at least once or twice. If you still don't know exactly what all the fuss is about you aren't alone, however, as a majority of Americans are still fuzzy on the details. The simple answer is that cryptocurrencies are a type of digital money that can be used in all the ways that traditional money can be and more. They are experiencing a massive boom at the moment thanks to a technology known as blockchain.

Blockchain technology is likely to come up in conversation when it comes to discussing smart contracts, Ethereum, bitcoin or cryptocurrency in general. Regardless of the specifics, the conversation is going to revolve around the fact that blockchain technology is useful when it comes to storing large amounts of primarily financial data in a database that is not accessible in a traditional centralized fashion. Blockchain technology has quickly become known for its extreme combination of security and accessibility.

Each individual block in the blockchain contains numerous different transactions as well as information that marks its unique place in the blockchain as a whole. When new information is added to the version of the blockchain that is connected to a specific node then that information is automatically transferred to all the other nodes in the system. When information is verified and added to the chain it automatically receives a timestamp as well so it is exceedingly easy to determine exactly when each transaction took place.

The auto-sorting nature of blockchain makes it possible for each to operate independently of all external control. Rather than a guiding hand, all of its processes are designed to take place automatically which means a single blockchain could easily be spread around the entire world and operate as if it were located in a single office. The nodes in the system then interact with one another via a means of specifically designed cryptography.

Blockchain technology allows for read access for users who have made transactions as well as write access for nodes. Users who can see but not touch are able to view their relevant transactions while nodes, and those with access to them, have the power to add new blocks to the chain directly. Blockchain security is so tight that it doesn't need to worry about actively combating external threats, instead its very nature ensures it is as secure as it is possible for a database to be given current technology limits.

Theoretical start

The concept that would eventually help to make blockchains a reality was used for the first time in the 1980s when it was first theorized as a means of preventing spammers from sending out unwanted emails. Known as a proof of work model, the basic idea, and one that is still at the heart of the verification process that blockchain systems use today, is that in order to send an email the sending computer would need to solve an equation that became infinitely more complicated the more emails the user tried to send at one time. Sending one email was easy, sending 10,000 was beyond the power of machines of the time.

This technology more or less lay fallow until the end of the last decade when discussion on a programming forum turned to the possibility of a digital currency that operated like cash in that it was completely autonomous to use. While most of the programmers in on the conversation were talking in the theoretical, one programmer who used the name Satoshi Nakamoto was ready to turn the talk into reality. Nakamoto soon released the concept and initial code that would go on to become the investment phenomenon known as bitcoin.

Once other developers bit on the open source code, the Nakamoto alias faded into the background, never to be heard from again. Not before mining the first bitcoin transaction, however, and sparking a cryptocurrency revolution.

To understand blockchain technology more readily, it is helpful to consider the way in which cryptocurrencies actually function. In general, they are a type of digital currency, that works the same way as any other online payment system. Where the differences come in, however, is the currency that is being traded in these transactions. While all previous types of digital transactions have been completed as a stand in for analog currency, cryptocurrency transactions exist purely in the digital space.

Each cryptocurrency gains value based upon what is agreed upon by the market as a whole and transactions that occur are then verified by third parties before being added to the blockchain directly. This verification is known as cryptocurrency mining and is done through the use of specialized hardware which is tuned to completed extremely complicated proof of work models as quickly as possible to verify the authenticity and accuracy of each individual transaction. Miners are then reward for their service with a small amount of the currency they are mining to offset their costs.

The global exchange rate for cryptocurrencies is known to vary drastically. However, since its creation, bitcoin has seen an unsteady, but undeniably strong, upward momentum from its original price of $.02.

2014 marked another exciting development for blockchain technology. Not only was bitcoin worth more than $1,000 for the first time and starting to catch on with mainstream investors in a big way, it was also when smart contracts were discovered. Perhaps it is more accurate to say that the ability to create smart contracts was created as before that the blockchain was only home to stagnant information. Not so anymore, however, as smart contracts are active code that can be injected into a block to carry out a specific task at a later date. The cryptocurrency platform known as Ethereum has since taken over the smart contract space in a big way.

Blockchain components

Database: When it comes to the differences between a blockchain database and a traditional database, the primary disparity is how latency is dealt with. With a centralized database, all of the information is kept as close to all the rest as possible in order to ensure that latency is kept to a minimum. Decentralized databases, on the other hand, don't care about latency at all, and in giving up on being latency free, they then become unencumbered enough to be spread out across any distance based on user need. With this sort of utilization method in place, blockchain allows currency to move about the same way that information does online.

Security: The cryptographic security surrounding blockchain is by far its most unique feature. This security comes from its decentralized nature as much as being a part of it. It works based on the self-sorting nature of all of the blocks in the chain. In order for a new block to be added to the chain successfully, all of the relevant information inside of it is going to have to be verified by all the other currently active nodes that are running the chain at that point and time. A full 51 percent of these nodes are going to have to confirm that the information provided is accurate before it will be accepted into the chain proper,

While this sounds pretty straightforward, what it means when it comes to cybersecurity is that the only way for false information to make its way into the blockchain is if more than 51 percent of all of the nodes running a particular blockchain would all need to be contaminated with false information at the same time. While it is not outside the realm of possibility for such a setup to occur, the cost and logistical requirements to do such a thing vastly outpace the potential for personal gain.

Relevant information: Each block contains the data that tells the location it maintains in the chain as a whole as well as the relevant transaction data that it was created to house in the first place. The transaction data takes up almost all of the available space so that after it is verified it moves through the nearest node and into the blockchain proper via a process called the best effort model. This model states that information is moved between relevant nodes based on which would require the smallest expense of additional energy. This is what allows the blockchain to work autonomously without a guiding force.

Verification: Once a new block is added to the chain, it is verified against the prime timeline and then given its proper place in the chain as a whole. After this occurs the blockchain then logs the block's relevant data and also verifies that its proof of work was completed properly to ensure the block was created in a legitimate fashion. As previously mentioned, these proof of work models require more computational power with each additional transaction that a blockchain contains which is why specialized machines are required in order to mine successfully.

Chapter 2: Understanding Cryptocurrency

Currently there are more than 1,000 different cryptocurrencies all competing to be the next bitcoin. All told, their combined market cap is approximately 60 billion dollars which puts them in the same general ballpark as companies like Tesla and Microsoft. With numbers like these it is easy to see why making the decision to learn more about cryptocurrency was clearly the right call.

A cryptocurrency is any type of digital currency that is purely based on computer code and cryptographic processes and relies solely on the market as a means of determining its value. Cryptocurrencies are tracked autonomously through the blockchain they are a part of and the sphere of influence that investors exert is enough to control it without the need for the governmental oversight that traditional forms of currency require. Bitcoin is the current leader in the space, while Ethereum is the alternative that is currently the closest to challenging its dominance. Despite this fact, many of the lesser known cryptocurrencies offer up a variety of strengths that could make them viable alternatives rather than simple also-rans.

While more traditional currencies are always going to be limited in their growth based on external values, cryptocurrencies generally run the gauntlet from less than a single cent all the way up to whatever bitcoin is worth when you are reading this. Broadly speaking, cryptocurrencies can be split into two types, those that are controlled by a centralized source, such as the currency that China has announced or those, like bitcoin, that are completely decentralized. The decentralized versions typically require more stringent verification methods in order to ensure that transactions easily get to where they need to be. Aside from the standard proof-of-work model, consensus protocols or consensus platforms can also be used.

Pricing

While cryptocurrencies don't have their prices controlled by a third party, that doesn't mean they aren't still bound by the laws of supply and demand. The price of a given cryptocurrency is always going to reflect the value the market assigns to it, which actually makes it a cleaner reflection of the concept than more traditional currencies. Likewise, just because there is no guiding hand, doesn't mean cryptocurrency prices aren't affected by external events. In fact, they are more likely to be affected by a wider array of situations as there is no limit to what might cause investors to sell.

When it comes to primary pricing influences, speculative investors play a much larger role in determining the current price of the cryptocurrency, especially when compared to more traditional currency types. This is especially true with smaller cryptocurrencies where there may only be a few thousand people holding it worldwide. Cryptocurrency trading works just the same as any other type of trading in that traders purchase a specific cryptocurrency that they hope will do well and the sell it when the opportunity to make a profit presents itself. When enough speculative investors buy into a specific currency and decide to hold then the result is that a pricing bubble starts to form. As the cryptocurrency market is already extremely speculative in nature it is particularly prone to this type of phenomena,

Pricing bubbles aren't all bad, however, at least as long as you managed to get in on the investment in question early enough to make a profit from the increasingly unrealistic price a bubble scenario with raise the cryptocurrency to. They are only really unfortunate for those who bought in late and decided to hold when it became clear that thinks weren't going to be turning around anytime soon.

It is also possible for external forces to combine in such a way that they can drive the price of a given cryptocurrency down, regardless of what the current level of demand might otherwise be. When this scenario occurs, it is not uncommon for the creators of the currency to attempt to take a more active role in the market process in hopes of stopping the downward trends in their tracks.

The first stop when it comes to changing public opinion is to increase the coverage of the cryptocurrency in question in the media. Increased coverage in the media is a great way for outside forces to manipulate the public by ensuring that they have something specific to focus on. Artificially generating public interest then typically leads to an almost immediate increase in price as late-to-the-party investor rush to jump on what they see as the next big thing. Common times for the media to take interest in a specific cryptocurrency include when it has been added to a new major cryptocurrency exchange, or when one which has been previously featured has a serious new update to its code. Additionally, the media loves a good soundbite or anything that shows the market for cryptocurrency is growing as a whole. Regardless of the context, the more people who hear the name of the cryptocurrency in question, the more the price will ultimately rise.

Having the right type of media coverage will go a long way towards changing the public's opinion about a specific cryptocurrency but it isn't going to do all of the work. This is mainly going to be done by the main proponents of the cryptocurrency in question. No matter how new a given cryptocurrency is, it is safe to assume that there is a vocal minority online that is willing to tell you why it is the greatest thing since sliced bread. These types of subgroups are often extremely useful when it comes to making moves that are likely to help to artificially inflate the price in question. What's more, this group of users will often work directly with the developers to improve the code for the cryptocurrency in addition to investing their own capital into it directly, all of which helps to increase its price overall.

A clear example of this occurred during the bitcoin bubble of 2014. Bitcoin was just months away from hitting $1,000 for the first time and traditional investors were starting to take notice. Despite having already been around for five years, bitcoin finally reached the level of mass adoption it required to spread word of mouth like wildfire and suddenly a currency that had previously just been used to buy drugs on the darknet was selling for more than $1,000 per coin.

Another way of taking advantage of online presence is through social media leaks. When traditional currencies are considering changing their interest rates, this news is often spread via traditional media channels, the same can be said with cryptocurrencies and social media. There are so many groups dedicated to cryptocurrency all across the internet that all it often takes to start a serious trend is to see the merest suggestion of news that would suggest the movement that the person who suggested the rumor was looking for. Oddly enough, this type of rumor mill typically ends up creating the very movement that it was predicting in the first place, regardless of whether the original rumor was true, or even an actually rumor.

Another common way these days to generate liquidity, one of the most important things to generating growth in the long-term for cryptocurrencies, is to generate automatic trades that are carried out by bots. This ensures that public interest remains stimulated and helps the price to remain at a steady rate. Liquidity relates to the amount of a given asset that is currently available to trade and if it is low then those looking to trade in a specific cryptocurrency won't have any means of purchasing it. As such, when the bots are deployed, their simulated transactions are then enough to often generate additional units of currency, thus improving liquidity overall. This practice is primarily prevalent in China where there are far fewer restrictions on what is and is not allowed in the cryptocurrency market. This has reached such epic proportions that China is actually responsible for a large number of bitcoins overall total liquidity.

Frequently, these tactics are used by those who have a vested interest in ensuring that the price of the cryptocurrency in question ends up as high as possible. This is often because they are trying to engage in a type of trading strategy known as a pump and dump. In this scenario, the investors buys up as much of the cryptocurrency in question as they can, before then going on to do everything in their power to ensure that the prices reaches as great of a peak as possible. Once they are sure that they aren't going to be able to squeeze anything else out of the market they then flood the market with the currency they purchased, dramatically dropping the price all at once

This is effective as cryptocurrency exchanges work through what are known as digital order books which generate lists of all the trades made and proffered in a single day. If the order book ends up being light on either buyers or sellers then the price will start to skew in a given direction. A pump and dump is much easier to pull off with cryptocurrency when compared to actual currency as the investor needs to control far fewer overall shares in order for it to be effective. Cryptocurrency exchanges all operate independently which means that the investor only needs to ensure that their chosen exchange ends up light on available units in order for the pump and dump to be successful.

Cryptocurrencies to watch

While bitcoin and Ethereum are at the top of the pile, there are many, many more cryptocurrencies you can explore if you are so inclined. The following list are some of the more interesting cryptocurrencies on the market today, but it is important to keep in mind that new cryptocurrencies are always coming online and the longer this book has been in the Kindle Marketplace, the less accurate the list is ultimately going to end up being. The following cryptocurrencies should be available on your favorite cryptocurrency exchange.

Litecoin: Litecoin is in many respects bitcoin 2.0, and that is clearly the impression it is trying to give off. It offers up much the same pitch as its clear inspiration except that its transaction times are much faster than what bitcoin can currently boast, cutting down on the potential for bottlenecking that is currently plaguing its namesake as well. It can process as many as five times the blocks as bitcoin can, though its methods are known to orphan blocks more frequently than bitcoin, though it also makes the potential for double-spending to occur much less likely as well. It is also known to require far less processing power when it comes to verifying litecoin transactions, as well as less when it comes to transactions fees. Payments speeds are also about four times that of what bitcoin is. There are currently about 84 million litecoins in the wild, which is about four times as many bitcoins that are left unmined. A single litecoin was worth about $40 in the summer of 2020.

Dogecoin: Dogecoin is either an example of how the internet can work together or a case of a meme going too far. It was first introduced as a joke in 2013, hence the Siba Inu dog that adorns its face. It quickly became more than that as the initial month of funding generated more than $60 million. A single dogcoin has gone on to be worth more than $1,000 and its users successfully crowdfunded a campaign to send a golden dogecoin to the moon in 2019. Currently there are more than five billion dogecoins produced each year and they are primarily used as a means of tipping internet comments for particularly useful or insightful content. Technically, dogecoin is also extremely on-point with a sub-60-seconnd processing time and no cap to the number of coins that can ultimately be generated overall.

Chapter 3: Cryptocurrency Trading

It is important to keep in mind that investing in cryptocurrency is going to be the right choice for everyone, however, and as such it is important to understand the various pros and cons of this investment opportunity before you commit to anything too enthusiastically.

The biggest pro comes in the added security that your personal information will experience when deal with cryptocurrency exchanges compared to traditional exchanges. Not only do you have the inherent security of blockchain technology keeping your personal details safe, in many instances you won't be required to divulge any personal information in order to get started trading cryptocurrency, especially if you already have some on hand to begin trading with. When you compare this type of operating setup to a traditional exchange, every single time that a transaction is made is another opportunity for someone to steal protected information.

This isn't even taking into consideration the ways in which digital currency is safer than physical currency. There is no way to forge a bitcoin or generate counterfeit dogcoins and once both parties have committed to a transaction there is no way that it won't go through as it is impossible to negate a transaction once it has been completed.

The other biggest benefit that cryptocurrency offers the world is the fact it means that anyone has access to traditional banking services. While this might not seem like that big of a deal to those where such things are common place, the fact of the matter is that nearly 50 percent of the world's population still doesn't have access to these types of services which means that once cryptocurrency becomes more common place it is going to make a serious difference in countless lives. As such, over the next five years, experts anticipate not just an increase in the everyday use of cryptocurrency, they anticipate a substantial increase. To understand just how significant the change is going to be, consider the fact that more people in Kenya right now have access to a bitcoin wallet than have access to sanitized drinking water.

Another reason that those in underdeveloped portions of the world are flocking to cryptocurrency is due to the fact that, despite the transaction fees involved, each cryptocurrency transaction frequently costs less than processing that same transaction through a traditional banking establishment. The same can be said about trades made via cryptocurrency exchanges which are often times as much as 50 percent cheaper than more traditional exchanges.

Everything is not all sunshine and roses with cryptocurrency technology, however, at least not yet. The biggest reason that this is the case is due to the fact that the technology surrounding blockchain and cryptocurrency in general is still so knew that it is literally impossible to determine just how it is all likely to shake out. For example, prior to 2014, the idea of smart contracts had never been seriously considered, but now, they are at the forefront of potentially useful blockchain adjacent technology. This means that while there are clearly already profits to be made, the potential for loss is literally unlimited until things begin to stabilize into a more long-term market.

This extreme level of uncertainty translates into a greater than average degree of volatility for all types of cryptocurrency. In fact, bitcoins are currently considered to be about three times more volatile than gold and four times more volatile than investments in the stocks of the S&P 500. As many early investors have learned, this high degree of volatility can directly translate into serious wins, but it can also translate into significant losses as well. Also affecting all cryptocurrency prices is the speculative bubble that they exist in. Currently, more than 75 percent of all cryptocurrency transactions are made for speculative purposes which means the bubble is bound to pop eventually. Only once cryptocurrencies are really being used for their intended purposes will the fear of bubbles become unfounded.

While the digital nature of cryptocurrency is often touted as a positive, it is important to consider its negative aspects as well. For example, as a purely digital construct, if you were keeping your cryptocurrency in an exchange that had a server error that resulted in a loss of all its backup drives, what would happen to your currency then? Likewise, what were to happen if you put your coins into a physical wallet that then stopped reading in your compute? Both of these cases are unlikely to happen, but if they were, then your cryptocurrency would be gone as if it had never existed in the first place. Furthermore, the massive potential for profits means that hackers are never going to stop trying to access these exchanges, so eventually they are going to succeed. When investing in cryptocurrency it is important to value security as highly as possible because there is very little standing between your investments and the void.

Making a good trade

In addition to being a potentially lucrative market, trading in cryptocurrency is a great choice for those who haven't spent much time trading previously because it differs from the standard method in several important ways. The first of these is that there are very few barriers to entry, getting started is as easy as finding an exchange you are interested in and trading your base currency for some cryptocurrency. Unlike the more unified traditional markets, each cryptocurrency exchange is independently owned which means the market is extremely fragmented. This leads to larger spreads then are commonly seen in most scenarios.

The lack of regulations around these organizations also means that the level of margin that you will be able to trade under is going to be larger than you can get just about anywhere else. Margin can lead to insurmountable losses, however, so it is important to avoid using it until you are very comfortable with the results you have been generating thus far. It is also worth pointing out that the prices for each exchange are going to vary somewhat based on personal supply which means that it is possible to find a cryptocurrency from one exchange and sell it for a profit on another bac k to back.

While every cryptocurrency is going to be subject to a price bubble of one sort or another, they are all going to be at varying levels which means it is quite likely you can get in early enough somewhere to ensure you turn a profit. Just be ready to keep an eye on how the bubble is progressing to ensure that you will be able to get out before it bursts and the price starts to drop extremely quickly.

When it comes to trading cryptocurrencies via a trading company, traders use what is known as a contract for difference. In this type of agreement, the seller and the buyer agree to a specific period of time. Once the timeframe expires, the buyer then payers the seller the difference between what the price was at originally, and the price now. If the difference is negative then the seller pays the buyer instead.

Picking an exchange

Another great thing about the cryptocurrency market is that the exchanges never sleep. It doesn't matter the time or the place, you can log on to an exchange and trade cryptocurrency with someone somewhere in the world. This is due to the fact that there are over 100 different exchanges around the world, all offering different currency pair and different rates, making it practically impossible to not find one that fits your particular needs and investment goals. This, coupled with the fact that virtually anything can set off a trend in either direction means that swings of five percent or greater are common with the cryptocurrencies and smaller exchanges can see changes of upwards of 20 percent in a single day.

Volatility like this is the reason it is so important to find an exchange that you can trust, as there is too much chance in the market already to add yet another thing to the list. As such, the first thing you are going to want to do when it comes to choosing an exchange is as much research as you can on the company itself and all its ins and outs. If you skip this step then you could conceivably end up in a scenario where your exchange closes up shop and takes your money with it in the process. If this occurs then it is unlikely that you are going to have much in the way or recourse which is why it is so important to choose wisely in the first place.

One of the most important traits for your cryptocurrency exchange to have is the level of transparency the exchange holds itself to for its day to day operations. This means you are going to want to take a look at their order book and also be provided with details such as where the company holds its funds and how their levels of reserve currency are verified. If these sorts of things are not readily available, and the company isn't extremely new, then there is likely a reason they prefer for this not to be the case. While this will not always be the case, exchanges that don't make all of their details public have the potential to be fractional exchanges which means they do not keep enough money on hand to satisfy all their debts to their clients at once. As such, if there was ever a reason everyone needed their money back at once, the exchange would run out of money and default. It should go without saying that fractional exchanges should be avoided at all costs.

Assuming their details are acceptable, the next thing you are going to want to research is the type of security that the exchange is utilizing when it comes to keeping your money safe. This means you are going to want to ensure that the site is running a secure HTTPS protocol as opposed to the more common HTTP. Additionally, it is important that in addition to requiring that you enter a password, they require that you utilize some form of dual-factor authentication. If you end up choosing an exchange with less than this level of security then all you are doing is putting your investment currency at risk.

As with their going rates for different cryptocurrencies, each exchange is going to have varying rates and fees associated with having an account with them. The amount that you are going to have to pay to have a transaction verified on the blockchain is going to stay the same, but what you are going to have the pay the exchange is going to vary based on either a flat per transaction rate or based on a portion of the transaction that was completed. This is not the case in China, however, where there are no exchange fees outside of what the blockchain charges to verify the transaction. Especially if you are trading on a regular basis, these fees can add up extremely quickly which means it is important to know what you are getting yourself into before you make a more official commitment.

In addition to the cost of each transaction, it is important to have a clear idea of just how long it is going to take between when you place your order and when it is going to be completed. The blockchain that the cryptocurrency that you are using is going to be a big part of this, as well as how many users are using the particular blockchain in the first place. A longer transaction time isn't inherently inferior to a longer one, as long as the exchange handles the delay in the right way. Specifically, it is important to ensure that your price is locked in when the transaction is placed, not when it is completed. If this is not the case then you could end up paying a dramatically different price depending on how long the transaction takes to process.

Finally, it is important to try and find a local exchange whenever possible. First and foremost, choosing an exchange in your own country dramatically increases the odds that, if your exchange does vanish, you will have some level of recourse. This is still far from a sure thing, however, but it is better than nothing. Furthermore, using a local exchange will make it easier for you to trade during peak times without having to get up in the middle of the night to do so. A word of warning however, just because an exchange is in a given country doesn't mean that it will take your native currency, double check before you make any commitments to save yourself an additional step every time you go to trade.

Exchanges to keep in mind

Bitstamp: This cryptocurrency exchange has been around longer than most others on the market today and was first started all the way back in 2011. It is the second most populated exchange and sees more than 10,000 units of currency move each day.

Bitfinex: The most commonly used exchange by a fair margin, Bitfinex moves more than

200,000 units of currency every single week. What's more, they offer new users who come in with cryptocurrency in hand the ability to start trading without any additional verification.

OKCoin: This is a Chinese coin that deals primarily in USD. This, as astute readers will remember, provides a wide variety of unique opportunities to USD holders who are looking for a few less rules standing between them and their trading.

Coinbase: This exchange has been operating continuously since 2010 which makes it the oldest continuously active exchange in the world. It is known for being extremely well regulated and even after all this time is still in the top five when it comes to average daily volume.

Initial offerings

If you spend any significant period of time trading in the cryptocurrency market, odds are that you will eventually catch wind of an ICO or initial coin offering. This is an increasingly common practice for blockchain based companies to finance their startup goals without having to apply for a traditional loan or use other crowdfunding tactics. This year alone, two companies have managed to raise more than $100,000,000 in less than 24 hours.

While the name comes from the more traditional initial public offering that occurs when a company issues stock for the first time, the two have relatively little in common. While IPOs provide those who bite the opportunity to own part of the company in question only offers early adopters the opportunity to purchase a new type of cryptocurrency at a low rate in hopes that it will increase to the point where doing so was a good decision. A majority of all ICOs these days are built on the Ethereum blockchain.

While a lot of the funding for these ventures comes from China, they by no means have a monopoly on the practice and investors worldwide are sure to bite if the terms are right. While investing in cryptocurrency in general is a high-risk proposition, investing in an ICO is even riskier still as it is functionally an unknown quantity. ICOs face several unique issues that make them a less than ideal investment choice starting with the fact that the companies that offer them aren't kept in check by rules from the SEC which means they are not held to any of the standards that an IPO must meet in order to move forward. Additionally, there are fears that any initial ICO success has just been a part of the larger cryptocurrency bubble and that success in this fashion is not feasible in the long-term.

While not without its potential issues, ICOs most assuredly have the potential to lead to serious profits for investors whose plans work out appropriately. Nevertheless, it is more important than ever in this instance to never invest more than you can afford to lose as there is a very real chance that you might. Before you go ahead and take the plunge, you are going to want to go ahead and ensure that you approach the ICO with the right mindset, right off the bat. This means digging into their available documentation including a business plan which will ensure that the company at least makes a basic level of financial sense before you start showering them with your hard-earned dollars and cents. It is also important that you only move forward with investments in which a proven need has been shown for the final product or service. Finally, don't forget to make sure that the cryptocurrency you are buying into will be a legitimate part of the final product and that you aren't being sold digital snake oil.

Unfortunately, when it comes to doing your research you are often going to be lucky to have a website, whitepaper and business plan to pull information from. As the company is unlikely going to have anything concrete to show off, you are taking on yet another risk by moving forward with this course of action. Furthermore, you are going to want to keep in mind that just because a company is seeing a strong response to their plan, doesn't mean that it will in any way translate into additional sales later on. Even worse, many analysts are of the opinion that giving a new company too much money too soon will only cause them to feel the need to spend it all while also minimizing the importance of actually producing a quality product because they are already seeing the fruits of their non-labor.

Last but not least, you will need to be leery of the fact that a majority of these companies are basing their entire business around the Ethereum platform as it is still a new technology and there is nothing to say that something better won't come along and replace it before a critical mass of acceptance has come along. Overall it is likely in your money's best interest if you wait to see if the initial round of ICOs pan out before investing in this direction.

Tips for success

Like many things in life, getting started trading and investing in the cryptocurrency market is relatively straightforward, finding success, however, can be much more complicated. Keep the following in mind to ensure you get started on the right foot.

Understand it is really just like any other commodity: From a market standpoint, cryptocurrencies are just like any other type of commodity. They are all used for more than just investing, precious metals are used for jewelry, base metals are used for industrial work and cryptocurrency is used as a means to conduct a wide variety of specialized transactions. Like other commodities, then, it is important to choose the right cryptocurrency to invest in based on how the practical application side of things is doing. It doesn't matter what speculative investors think in the long run, only true market demand will win out in the end.

Understand mass usage is coming: Cryptocurrency currently has an estimated $60 billion market cap despite the fact that much of the world still has very little idea what it is exactly, just imagine what that number is going to be once things really get up and rolling. Every day, more and more people are learning about blockchain and cryptocurrency technology is and how it can affect their lives for the better. As this increasingly becomes the norm, more and more services are going to release to the public and as these services become easier to use, usage rates will eventually hit mass adoption numbers. Analysts predict that this will happen around 2022 and it is at this time that the bubble surrounding cryptocurrencies will likely burst for the last time.

The market cycle is important: The market cycle is a useful means of looking at the way all investments follow the same pattern when given a long enough timeline for doing so. The market cycle for cryptocurrency in general is currently in the optimism phase which means that next will thrill followed by euphoria which can never be sustained which is why it is followed by anxiety, denial, fear, depression and finally panic as the price hits a point of freefall. Things then eventually right themselves and depression gives way to hope, relief and optimism.

Bitcoin has already been through this cycle once before, when it bottomed out during the crash in 2014, most of the rest are still in the optimism stage, however, which means there is still plenty of opportunity to take advantage of years of investor goodwill as long as you take advantage of the market sooner than later. With the right research, and a little luck, you could easily see steady returns for at least five years before you need to start worrying if your cryptocurrency is going to survive the impending fallout. Much like the dotcom boom of the late 90s, once the bubble bursts roughly 80 percent of all cryptocurrencies are going to go bust while the market adapts to the new major players on the scene.

Expect success in the long-term: While bitcoin saw growth of nearly $2,000 over the summer of 2020, those types of results are far from typically which means that if you want to plan on making money from cryptocurrency you need to plan on doing so over the long-term. It is early days for the cryptocurrency market as a whole which makes the potential for exceptional deals so readily available, this won't last forever, however, so getting in soon is recommended for the best results.

However, unlike investing in other types of securities, investing in cryptocurrency doesn't involve any type of lock-in risk whatsoever as they can easily be exchange for other types of currency at the drop of the hat instead of locking you in to a scenario where you need to rely on a third part to ensure a return on your investment. This means you can essentially use investing in cryptocurrency as a form of high return savings account.

Keep an eye on Ethereum

While bitcoin is definitely still at the top of the pile, it is no longer the type of hot new investment that it was a few years ago which means there are likely better alternatives when it comes to seeing the maximum amount of profit possible. No, the holder of that title is the Ethereum platform, and the currency known as ether. It has already seen about half as many transactions as bitcoin, despite only being around for a third of the time and is more firmly focused on the future with its improved interactions with smart contracts and its decentralized app platform as well.

Perhaps more importantly, if you look at the transaction chart for bitcoin then you will see that it is nothing but peaks and valleys. It's true that things tend to move in an overall positive direction, but it can hardly be called steady growth. On the contrary the Ethereum chart shows a much more overall bullish outlook, even through the summer of 2020 when blockchain was at its current peak.

It is important to keep in mind that cryptocurrencies are always going to be social constructs which means that Ethereum's robust network effects make it easier for the network, and its value, to continue to grow steadily moving forward.

This is crucial for several reasons, the first of which is that the bitcoin blockchain has already reached a point where it can't handle any more peak usage. The bitcoin blockchain processes roughly 7 transactions each second which means that at the moment there are more than three million transactions that are sitting and waiting for the blockchain to catch up. This means that the blockchain would need to process transactions for about a week, just to catch up to where it needs to be right now. This isn't caused by any one factor so much as the fact that the blockchain is nearly a decade old and new technology has eclipsed it in virtually every way.

This, coupled with the way the platform has embraced smart contracts means that a majority of the leading developers in the blockchain space are currently in the process of shifting their products to the Ethereum blockchain. Ethereum is also capable of far more transactions per second and the fees for each is going to be lower as well. Experts are already expecting Ethereum's user base to grown ten-fold in 2018.

It is also important to keep in mind that many of the applications that are currently n development are going to focus on making the cryptocurrency experience more user friendly and something that the average person will be able to natively intuit. As these projects start to come online, they will cause usage rates to continue to rise and push Ethereum to the forefront of many peoples' minds when they think of blockchain or cryptocurrency technology at all.

5 Trading Mistakes to Avoid

For most, trading can be challenging, regardless of their experience level. Trading strategy, emotions, and analysis all play an important role when it comes to doing your best.

However, more often than not, a trader will end up making some sort of mistake. No matter your experience level, the following are the five most common mistakes made by traders.

Tops and Bottoms: The interest in grabbing a bottom or top is tempting. There is a large appeal in a contrarian market approach, but unless there is a really good reason, lock in your profits before the top of a top or bottom of a bottom.

The main reason why a trader will chase the tops and bottoms is the psychology. Traders think that the market, especially right after a strong trend, will change to enter into a new trend. This can lead a trader into taking a bad position. The fact is that trends can only be validated when the price has moved considerably from its support or resistance level and even the best traders or analysts will find it extremely hard to call a bottom or top. To ensure you do not fall prey to chasing tops and bottoms, you have to set your impulses and emotions aside and look at the market objectively.

Trying to pick a top or bottom is common, but it has an equally large risk. Traders should turn to other strategies like Bolinger Bands, high-low methods, or divergence. These are helpful in predicting when the momentum will be exhausted.

Bad Risk Management: The interesting thing is that, for the most part, traders tend to be correct in their analysis. What they tend to get wrong is their money management. Entering a big position quickly because your analysis shows that the prices will probably turn may end up leaving you at risk of the prices continuing to grow.

When you have too much first position exposure, it may become difficult to manage your trade goes wrong. There are two golden rules that every trader should follow.
1. Always expect your first position to be wrong and use a smaller first position.
2. Increase your position when your first position is proven to be correct.

These two rules will enable you to think critically, lower your losses and increase profits. Review these rules every month to ensure they set into your trading plan.

Allowing Losses to Pile Up: One of the most important characteristics of a successful trader is being able to get out of a position with a small loss quickly if they see a trade is not going to work out and they then move onto the next trade. On the other hand, the unsuccessful trader will become paralyzed if their trade goes against them. Instead of acting quickly to cap their loss, they tend to hold their position in the hopes of the trade working out. In addition to tying up their capital for a long period of time and becoming a bag holder, this type of inaction could cause mounting losses and depletion of their capital.

Failure to Make Use of Stop-Loss Orders: This is a mistake linked to the one above. To be successful in trading, you have to have use stop-loss orders. The failure to implement this one is the worst mistake that you can make. A tight stop-loss typically means that a loss will be capped before they become too large. A 10% stop-loss below your buy price is usually sensible. So if you invest $100 you can only lose a maximum of $10 returning you majority of your capital.

Not Sticking to or Not Creating a Trading Plan: Experienced traders always need to have a trading plan. The plan will help traders know when they will enter and exit, how much they will invest, and the max loss they will take. A novice trader may end up not having a plan before they start trading. Even if they have come up with a plan, they are more likely to abandon it than the more experienced traders if they think things are not going to plan.

Avoiding the above mistakes can preserve your capital and mitigate your risk when entering into the world of Cryptocurrency trading. Cryptocurrency is an extremely volatile asset and can deplete your funds very quickly if the correct measure are not taken. Conversely, if they are implemented with a good trading plan the rewards are immense.

Chapter 4: Mining

If trading or investing in cryptocurrency doesn't sound like it is going to be for you but you still want to make money off this whole cryptocurrency thing sooner rather than later, then cryptocurrency mining might be more your speed. Every cryptocurrency whose blockchain uses the SHA-256 double round hash process when it comes to verifying transactions uses the same basic mining process when it comes to keeping the blockchain safe and secure from external threats. In exchange for mining, miners receive a predetermined amount of the cryptocurrency in question for their help which goes to offsetting costs and also making the entire process worth your time.

The greater the processing power of the machine you use, which is measured in terms of hashes per second, the more likely you will be to complete proof of work models and the more you stand to make as a result. The most commonly used proof of work model is known as the hashcash model which is a type of cryptographic algorithm which utilizes a hash function at its core. Hashcash proofs can then be set to a specific difficulty in order to ensure that blocks are not created faster than the blockchain can handle which means it needs to be set based on the number of transactions that can be successfully processed per second. For example, a new bitcoin block is only created every 10 minutes. The probability of successful generation is quite low so it is practically impossible to determine when a specific machine will generate a new block.

In order for that block to be seen as valid, the hash value it uses needs to great than that of the block which came before it which means that each block naturally contains the work that was done to create it. Each block then also contains the hash of the proceeding block which is how the chain determines where exactly each individual block belongs. This means that it is impossible to change a single block without redoing the work that has been done on every proceeding block.

Get into the mining game

The best mining machine and the best price that you can expect to pay for it is something that changes regularly which means that some additional research is going to be required in order to determine what is currently state of the art. The best place to find out new up-to-the-moment information is going to be on the subreddit for the currency you are considering mining. Once you know what you are looking for, odds are you will be able to find a version of it on Amazon.com.

While the specifics of the system you end up with are going to vary based on the times, one thing that is never going to change is that you will need dedicated hardware in order to mine cryptocurrency effectively. While it is technically still possible to mine with a computer's video card or a laptop's CPU, the speed with which modern mining machines can complete proof of work transactions means that you would be unlikely to finish a single verification in a year's time.

ASIC is the company that is known to produce the best products and tend to offer speeds that are roughly a hundred times more than what the average computer can manage. In general, trying to mine without specialized software is going to end up costing you more in electricity than you will end up making on the endeavor. As of fall 2017, the average mining machine costs between $500 and $4,000 with pricier machines resulting in a higher payout.

Once you have a machine in hand, the next thing you are going to need to do is to download the relevant mining software. There are numerous different versions of this software available, and not all are compatible with all types of cryptocurrency, so it pays to look into the specifics of your desired cryptocurrency before committing to anything. The most popular versions of the software include CGminer and BFGminer, or EasyMiner for those who aren't comfortable running software from the command line.

Once you have the required software in place, the next thing you will need to do is find a mining pool to join so that you can maximize your potential mining power. A mining pool is a collection of miners that have joined together in order to ensure that they can mining as many blocks as possible. Like owning a dedicated mining machine, joining a mining pool is technically optional, though the complexity of the average proof of work model is such that joining is really the best way to make in money off the process. When working with a mining pool you will receive a portion of the profits from every block that your machine helps to verify as determined by one of several different compensation models.

If you do decide to set out on your own, you will need to download the core client for the blockchain that you will be interacting with as it is required to ensure your version of the blockchain is synced up with the blockchain prime. This can generally be found on the primary website for the cryptocurrency you are going to be working with. If you are planning on joining a pool instead, then all you need to do is ensure that you follow any instructions that the pool sends your way and do your best to keep your behavior in line with any guidelines.

There are a wide variety of different types of mining pools in the validation space these days which can make finding the right one for you something of a chore. In order to simplify the process as much as possible, the first thing that you are going to want to do is to research the pools you are considering on the relevant subreddit. Doing so will ensure that you can read about each of the pools before you commit to anything and prevent you from signing on with a lemon. While joining a popular pool will often mean you are eligible for more blocks, the amount you get from each will be lower than if you choose a smaller pool. It is typically considered to be better for the health of a particular blockchain if users mine in larger numbers of smaller pools to guarantee that enough proofs are always being generated.

When looking into various pools, you will need to look carefully at any content provided when it comes to how payment is generated as this is a much more complicated process than it may initially appear. There are countless different payment methods and you would do well to be familiar with the most frequently used varieties to ensure you don't end up with something that you won't like in the long-term.

Pay per share: The pay per share (PPS) model pays miners for their share of the work as soon as the block has been verified with a specific amount for each portion of the proof that their machine generated. Miners are paid out for their work from the pool's total holdings, without waiting for the payment to be processed by the blockchain. This structure is preferred by miner's as it ensures there is very little variance in what each block will generate in profits and it puts all the risk in case something goes wrong onto the pool operator. As there is always a risk that a block will not payout and will instead be orphaned, the operator then runs the risk of not being paid for the work in the long run after having already paid the miners out from the pool's funds. Additionally, the operator is required to have a lot of excess capital on hand to ensure that they can continue to remain solvent during slow periods. Due to these reasons, the PPS model is not as common as it once was.

Proportional approach: The proportional mining approach distributes mining rewards based on the portion of the block that their machine provided. Payments are then generated after payments have been generated for the block in question.

Pay per last N share: The pay per last N Share (PPLN) model is similar to the proportional method except instead of true shares it generates profit margins based on N shares. The difference between it and a PPS model is that an N share pays out a variable rate based on how much was rewarded from the block in question which means the amount each miner receives is always going to vary based on the results. Payments are then sent out after the reward for the block have been received.

Double geometric: The double geometric payment method is a type of hybrid approach to mining payments that splits the risk between the pool operator and the miners. The pool operator then takes a portion of the profits when things are going well and uses those funds to pay miners when things aren't going according to plan. Payments made through this system are generated based on shares and payments are made once a block is successfully added to the chain.

Shared maximum pay share: The shared maximum pay share model (SMPPS) is an updated version of the PPS model that sees more use these days because of the way it mitigates risk for the pool operator. It offers up a reward per share amount that is based on how much the pool has earned in the recent past. Payments are made on a predetermined schedule assuming all relevant blocks have been accepted into the chain.

Recent shared maximum: The recent shared maximum pay per share model (RSMPSS) is another variation on the PPS model that prioritizes newer pool members so they are more likely to receive a greater number of shares compared to those who have been in the pool the longest. Payments are made at set intervals after all the verified blocks have been successfully added to the chain.

Capped pay per share and back pay: The capped pay per share with recent back pay model of payment (CPPSRB) is a variation of the standard MPPS payment method that pays miners as much as possible based on the rewards generated while ensuring that the pool remains solvent first and foremost. Payments are then sent out after the reward for the block have been received.

Pooled mining model: The pooled mining model (PMM), more commonly known as the slush pool, is a type of payment model where the final shares of a given proof of work model are given a better rate when compared to earlier shares which are naturally easier to generate. This payment model is especially effective when it comes to stopping miners from dropping out of a job after the halfway point when the rewards are fewer compared to the work that is being completed. Payments are then sent out after the reward for the block have been received.

Pay on target: The pay on target (POT) payment method is yet another PPS variation except that this one pays out individual miners based on the resources each one used to generate the proof of work model as a whole. Payments are then only generated on a set schedule after the relevant blocks have all been verified.

SCORE: The SCORE payment model uses a specialized reward system that weighs shares differently based on how quickly the block was mined overall. It also pays more for later shares of any block to compensate for the additional resources required to complete it successfully. Payments are then generated based on the scores that each miner received during the proof. Payments are sent out after the reward for the block have been received.

Eligius: The eligius model of payment was created by the owner of BFG miner in an effort to improve upon the standard PPS model. It uses the strengths of the PPS model along with those of the BPM model to create a payment model that allows miners to be paid for their work right away. Each miner is paid out based on an equation that takes the total reward for a given block and then divides the amount evenly by all the shares that were used to generate the block, while also calculating any users who have shares of stale blocks in the current proof as well. Miners who end up with a stale block then have those shares rolled over into the next successfully completed block they are a part of.

Chapter 5: Creating a Personalized Trading Plan

No single investing strategy is going to be right for everyone because every investor is going to have different reasons for wanting to invest, different levels of comfort when it comes to risk, different timeframes for doing so and different metrics for success. As such, in order to create a truly personalized trading plan it is important to consider several different factors about your own life first.

Consider trading goals

First, it is important to determine the goals you have when it comes to investing which can be done by first asking yourself what your objectives are when it comes to investing. For some people, safely maintaining their principle investment will be enough, while others will be trying to accumulate money for a long-term goal.

Depending on your goals for investment you may even want to go ahead and create different investments for different goals. Regardless, before you go ahead and invest it is important to have a clear idea of the reasons you are doing so to make it easier to determine the best way to go about reaching the goal you are seeking.

Finally, it is important to keep in mind that goals should not be completed in a vacuum; you will also need to keep in mind your desired timeframe and level of risk tolerance in order to make goals that are realistically achievable.

Consider your risk tolerance

Before you can accurately determine your goals, it is important to consider your overall tolerance for risk, specifically the risk of losing money. The basics of determining the amount of risk you are comfortable with involve considering how much money you would be willing to risk and still be okay with not receiving any profit and even possibly having that amount be reduced to zero.

It is important to keep in mind that all investment involves risk and without some level of risk there can be no profit. The amount of risk that you are going to be able to deal with is likely going to be, in part, about how soon you need to see a return on your investment. If you are saving for retirement and have 20 or more years to go before the day arrives then you will be able to make riskier investments than someone who is already in their sixties who will naturally have a much lower level of risk as a result.

Consider trading limits

Once you are aware of your relationship to risk, you will then need to establish trading limits, both for trades that have soured as well as those that are going along as planned. This upper limit is what is known as a price target which can be thought of as the best-case scenario for the investment you are currently tracking. This is the number that you will be happy with taking the profits from, even if the price continues to move past that point in a positive direction.

A price target can be thought of as your expectation for how the cryptocurrency in question is going to move in the short-term which means it might have numerous different price targets depending on who is doing the trading and their personal feelings about the cryptocurrency in question. There is no one right price target it is purely based on what is right for you.

Consider your ideal level of involvement

Once you know how adverse to risk you are, you will also need to consider how active you are going to want to be in your investments. If you are comfortable holding onto specific investment for a prolonged period of time while only checking in on it occasionally then you are most likely going to want to pursue a buy-and-hold strategy, where relatively reliable investments are going to return reliable, if unimpressive, returns. If you are more interested in micromanaging your investments, then you can pursue riskier investments that have a greater potential for large payouts, but you might need to bounce between several different investments as needed. In general, you should not pursue a daily trading strategy unless you are a professional.

Consider your familiarity with trading

When it comes to creating a trading plan that is sure to lead to success, the first thing that you will want to consider is your overall familiarity with the ins and outs of trading in general, and higher risk trading in particular. The greater your overall experience level, the more ambitious your plan and your trades can be, but there is no shame is sticking with the basics if you are just getting started overall. When it comes to determining your personal skill level, it is important to be honest with yourself as overestimating your abilities is only going to come back to haunt you later on when you end up in over your head with more than you can realistically afford to lose on the line.

Consider your strengths and weaknesses

Next, you will need to determine how knowledgeable you are in the arena you are investing in as well as your overall level of comfort when it comes to monitoring your investments and making decisions based on their future. Your investment decision should be based around your comfort level and your willingness to devote time to researching your choices. Finally, it is also important to be frank with yourself when it comes to knowing what you don't know. Never let yourself be talked into investing in something that you aren't comfortable with or don't understand and never invest more than you can afford to lose no matter how good the deal might seem on the surface.

Consider the other challenges in your life at the moment

Once you know what personal hurdles you are going to have to overcome, the next thing that you will need to do is to consider the other facets of your life and make note of things that might make it more difficult than it otherwise might be to day trade successfully. External challenges are often things like a weak starting fund, other time commitments or anything else that will prove difficult when it comes to planning out the perfect trade strategy. The exact issues are going to be different for everyone, but knowing what they are is half of the battle. The market is inconsistent enough, don't try and come at it without having all of the other possible variables on lock.

Stick with it

In order to determine if your plan is successful, the first thing you are going to need to do is give it some time to generate real results. Based on the time frame for profit you determined previously, you are going to want to wait and gather enough data to ensure that you are likely to turn a profit using your plan in the long-term. During this time, you are going to want to take detailed notes including when trades were made, what factors went into your consideration for the trades, the costs and if the trade ended in success. Keep in mind that anything above 50 percent will eventually turn a profit given a lengthy enough timeframe.

Most importantly, if you find a trading plan that works for you, you are going to want to stick with it as diligently as possible, even if your emotions are telling you to go a different way. When trading, your goal should always be to minimize the effect that emotions have on your actions as completely as you can. Trading successfully is all about the numbers which means that emotions are only going to get in the way and almost always end up doing you more harm than good. The more robotically you can execute the trades you are looking for, the greater your profits are going to be across the board. If you find yourself considering making a trade based on emotion, take a moment to ask yourself if you would make the trade if your emotions weren't a factor and then make a choice depending on the answer.

Don't be too anxious to get started

In order to trade successfully, it is important that you start off on the right foot which means having enough trading capital to push through the early days when you are more likely to make a poor decision. If every trade, you make represents the difference between continuing to trade and having to go back to a traditional 9-to-5 then you are likely to be more focused on this fact as opposed to making the best trades possible and sticking with your trading plan. This, in turn, will make it more likely for you to trade based on fear rather than anything truly rational such as what the market is currently telling you is the right thing to do.

It is important to always be aware of your personal limits when it comes to trading both mentally and in regard to trading capital, but it is equally important to not have to deal with such strict limits that you chafe under them and fail to trade properly as a result. Remember, no trader is ever going to be 100 percent successful which means that if you hope to play the long game you need to be able to survive long enough for your plan to work out in the long run.

Chapter 6: Trading Strategies to Try

Long Position

Long position is when you buy a Cryptocurrency with the intent that it will go up in value. When an investor or trader makes a long position investment, they purchase Cryptocurrency and hold it hoping that the price will go up. They typically do not have a plan to sell their coin until they see the price of Cryptocurrency rise till their desired taking target is reached. An important part of long position investment is owning a Cryptocurrency. This is different from a short position investment, where the investor never owns Cryptocurrency, but, instead, borrows it and expects to sell it and then buy it at a cheaper price. One of the biggest differences between long and short position trading is what the trader thinks will happen to the coin's price.

Short Position Trading

A trader can short Cryptocurrency. Short selling is typically conducted through a margin account which will be discussed. Shorting is a very risky strategy and should only be attempted when a trader develops an intuition of the market and long trading experience.

A trader will go long on Cryptocurrency when they expect the price to increase, but a trader will go short if they anticipate that the price will fall. Short selling gives you the chance to sell something that you do not own. A short seller can do this by borrowing Cryptocurrency from a broker or exchange and then selling at the current market price. What they make from the sale will go to the seller's margin account. The seller will cover their position by buying the same number of Cryptocurrency on the market when the price has decreased and then repaying their debt back to the broker or exchange.

The purchase price and sale price difference it what gives the seller their profit or loss. For example, you could short 10 Cryptocurrency at $15,000 per coin. Thereafter, the price declines to only $12,000. At this point, you then buy 10 Cryptocurrency back. The gross profit for this short is $30,000. The net profit will be lower, owing to the fees and interest that is involved with margin trading.

Trading Analysis

Cryptocurrency traders have a number of tools at their fingertips to evaluate the market; one of the most common, and most used methodologies is technical analysis. When traders use this approach, they receive a better read on market sentiment and use these tools to figure out the key trends, and with all of this information, they can make better predictions.

Technicians, or chartists, take a more practical approach. They look at the history of Cryptocurrency and will apply several different analytical tools to see where the market goes.

Fundamental analysis, which is the opposite of technical analysis, is more about figuring out what Cryptocurrency should be worth, chartists or technical traders only look at the real price movements. When you look at the history of Cryptocurrency's price, the main pattern to find is price resistance and price support. This book will only cover technical analysis as Cryptocurrency has an inherent worth of being the cryptocurrency with first mover advantage, the primary trading pair and the currency with the biggest market capitalization by day and overall trading cementing its position as the master digital currency.

Bullish and Bearish Markets

The market is known as bullish when it is believed that the price of a stock or

Cryptocurrency will go up. When an investor believes that the price will go up, they will buy calls. They will have paid for the right to buy a stock a certain price, which is referred to as strike price or exercise price. An investor is considered bullish if they sold puts. When an investor sells a put, they are obligated to buy the stock, which means they likely believe the price will go up.

The market is known as bearish when it is believed that the price of Cryptocurrency will fall. When an investor sells a call, they are obligated to sell their stock to the buyer at a certain price. They do this because they believe that the price will fall. An investor who buys a put is looking for the price to fall so that they can sell the stock at a better price to the person who sold the put.

Volume

Cryptocurrency traders need to consider that volume plays a huge role in assessing price trends. High volume whether hourly or daily shows you there is a strong price trend, and low volume tells you there are weaker trends. If the price of Cryptocurrency was to experience a large loss or gain, a trader needs to make sure that they examine the volume.

If Cryptocurrency had a long uptrend and then it suddenly declined, it would be worth checking the volume to figure out if this downward movement is showing a new trend, or if it is a temporary pullback.

A price increase will typically coincide with a volume increase. If the price of Cryptocurrency was to experience an uptrend, but the upward movement happened during weak volume, this might mean that the trend is losing steam and may end soon.

Charts

Even if you have not previously given it much thought, you have likely seen a common pricing chart at one point or another. As the name implies, it simply shows the movement of the price of a given asset, over a set period of time. There are charts based on a wide variety of intervals from those that show movement by the minute, all the way to those that show it by the year.

Candlesticks

Candlestick charting appeared around 1850. The credit for developing candlestick charting goes to a rice trader Homma who lived in Sakata. More than likely his ideas were refined and modified from many years of trading and eventually, the results were the charts we use now.

To make a candlestick chart, you must have data that contains close, low, high, and open values for all the time periods you might want to display. The portion that is hollow or filled is called the body. The thin lines that are above or below show the high or low range. These are called shadows, tails or wicks, all used interchangeably. The high gets marked by the top of the top wick and the low by the lower wick. If the price of Cryptocurrency closes higher than it was when it opened, a hollow candlestick is drawn at the bottom indicating the opening price and the top indicating the closing. If the stock closes lower than when it opened, a filled candlestick is drawn at the top indicating the opening price and the bottom indicating the closing.

When it gets compared to normal bar charts, most traders think that candlestick charts are easier to read and look better. Each candlestick will show a way to figure out the price action. A trader can compare the relationship of the opening and closing as well as the highs and lows. The relationship between the opening and closing is vital information that shows the significance of the candlesticks. Hollow ones will show buying pressure. This is when the closing is bigger than the opening. Filled candlesticks will show selling pressure. This shows the closing was less than the opening.

Long green candlesticks show strong buying pressure. The longer the candlestick, the farther the closing was about the opening. This will show that the price grew more from opening to closing and buyers were aggressive. Long green candlesticks are bullish indicating an upward trend. After long declines, a long green candlestick might mark a turning point. If buying becomes extremely aggressive after a long advance, it could lead to greater bullishness.

Long red candlesticks show a large selling pressure. The longer the candlestick, the farther the close was from the opening. This will show that prices went down from the opening and sellers were very aggressive in selling. After a long advance, this candlestick could indicate a turning point or mark where a resistance level might be in the future. After a decline, a red candlestick shows capitulation or panic.

Wicks on candlesticks provide significant information about the session. Upper wicks indicate the highs and the lower wicks indicate the lows of that session. Candlesticks that have short wicks indicate that most of the actions were close to the opening and closing prices.

Candlesticks with long wicks indicate prices went far past the opening and closing of that session whether it be an hour or a day.

Candlesticks that have long upper shadows and short lower shadows indicate that buyers had control of the session and bid high. Sellers forced the prices down later from the high, and the close being weak made long upper shadows. This can indicate strong short trading activity.

Candlesticks with long lower shadows and short upper shadows indicate sellers were in control of the session and caused the prices to go lower. Buyers came back later to cause the prices to go high near the end of the session. The strong close created a long lower shadow. This usually indicates FOMO (fear of missing out) activity.

Candlesticks that have long upper shadow, a long lower shadow, and a small body are called spinning tops. A long shadow indicates a reversal. Spinning tops indicate indecision. The small body that is either filled or hollow indicates insignificant movement from opening to closing. The shadows indicate that both bears and bulls were active. The session could have opened and closed with little change or prices might have moved higher or lower during the session. If sellers or buyers do not have the upper hand, the result is a standoff. After a long advance, a spinning top indicates weakness with bulls and an interruption of the trend. Once a decline is over, a spinning top shows weakness with bears and an interruption of the trend. This indicated where price activity is flat and is quite boring and unprofitable for traders.

Candlesticks give valuable information on the positions of the opening, highs, lows, and closing. This activity makes all candlesticks differ.

Bullish reversals need preceding downtrends while bearish reversals need prior uptrends. The direction is figured by using trend lines, moving averages, peat/through analysis and other technical analysis tools. A downtrend might come about if the Cryptocurrency is trading below the downtrend line, below the previous high, or below a moving average. Since candlesticks relate to a certain period of time selected by the user, it is best to consider price action by analyzing the historical candlesticks to determine future price movement.

A candlestick that is away from the previous candlestick is in the star position. The first will have a large body; the second will have a small body. It will depend on the previous candlestick. The star position could gap up or down, and it looks to be isolated from the former price action. The candlestick could be any combination of red or green. Spinning tops, shooting stars, hammers, and dojis have small bodies that could show up in the star position.

Moving Averages
A great technique for Cryptocurrency traders to use to find trends is moving averages. This technique helps smooth out the currency's fluctuations so that the participants can better understand where the price is going.

The basic type of moving average is 'simple moving average.' This is figured out by calculating the security's average price over a certain period of time. A trader could choose to look at what Cryptocurrency has done over a 50, 100 or 200 day/hourly period. Cryptocurrency being such a strong cryptocurrency usually finds resistance on the 50 day/hour moving average on a daily basis but can drop to the 100 day/hour average. If the price of Cryptocurrency falls below that it could signify a temporary bearish trend.

Another tool that these traders could use is 'exponential moving average.' This provides more of an emphasis on the recent price values when looking at the average. By analyzing the averages, a trader can better understand when the momentum tends to shift. If the price of Cryptocurrency crosses the 21 day/hour average and ends up falling below a 51 day/hour average, this may point to bearish movement. The converse is true if you were to see that the shorter average is moving higher than, the longer average.

RSI: The relative strength index (RSI) is typically used to calculate results in increments of three days and measures the total sum of positive days and negative days before calculating a value with a range between 0 and 100. If the movement of the cryptocurrency in this period is generally positive, then the indicator will end up closer to 100 and if the movement is negative the result will be closer to 0. As such, if the result is close to 50 then the results are considered to be neutral.

MACD: Moving average convergence divergence (MACD) is a type of trend following momentum indicator that expounds upon the relationship between two different averages and prices. The MACD can be determined by taking the 26-day EMA and subtracting the 12-day EMA from it.

MACD can be interpreted in multiple ways. The first of which is the crossover. When the MACD falls underneath the signal line then this creates a bearish signal that says it is time to sell. Alternately, if the MACD is above the signal line then it shows that the price of the underlying asset is about to experience upward momentum. It is common for traders to wait for a confirmed cross that is above the signal line before making a move based on the position in order to ensure that the price isn't going to go through a fake out phase.

Stochastic: The stochastic oscillator is a type of momentum indicator which compares the closing price of an underlying asset to the range of prices it achieved over a specific period of time. The sensitivity of this oscillator to specific movements of the market can be reduced by adjusting the time period or through the process of taking a moving average of its results.

The stochastic oscillator also plays an important role when it comes to determining if a specific underlying asset is oversold or overbought due to the fact that it remains range bound. Its range is between 0 and 100 and will always remain constant regardless of how quickly or slowly the underlying asset moves.

The traditional setting for this oscillator is 20 as the oversold threshold with the overbought threshold appearing at 80.

A/D Line: The Advance-Decline (A/D) Line is an indicator for breadth that takes into account net advances which is the number of cryptocurrencies that are seeing gains when compared to those who are seeing losses. The line can then be used to compare the expected performance of the market as a whole compared to how it is actually doing. When bearish or bullish divergences are found in the A/D line then it is a signal that a reversal could be on the horizon.

Ichimoku Clouds: The Ichimoku cloud pattern is a type of trend trading and charting system that is purpose-built to be useable in virtually every trading market. It has several unique characteristics, but its primary strength lies in the fact that it utilizes multiple different points of data as a means of giving the trader using it a comprehensive view of the current price action. This more insightful view, coupled with the fact that it is a very visual system in general, makes it easy for traders to quickly separate potential trades with a low probability of success from those that are more likely to work out in the end.

The Ichimoku chart is made up of 5 different indicator lines, a brief summary of each and how it is calculated is outlined below:

- Tenkan Sen: This is the turning line and it is determined by adding together the lowest low and the highest high, and then dividing the result by 2 for the previous 9 periods.

- Chikou Span: This is the lagging line and it is calculated by taking the current closing price and then time-shifting it backwards 26 periods.

- Kijun Sen: This is the standard line and it is determined by adding together the lowest low and the highest high before diving the result by 2 for the previous 9 periods.

- Senkou Span A: This is the first leading line and it is determined by adding together the tenkan sen and the kijun sen, dividing by two and then shifting the result forward by 26 periods.

- Senkou Span B: This is the second leading line and it is determined by that the sum of the lowest low and the highest high, dividing by 2 for the previous 52 periods and then taking the result and shifting it forward 26 periods.

CCI: The Commodity Channel Index (CCI) is an indicator that can be useful when it comes to determining new trends or determining when extreme market conditions are forthcoming. It measures the current level of the price relative to the average over a specific period of time. The CCI will remain high when prices are greater than average and low if the price is beneath where the market would naturally indicate it should be.

Bollinger Bands: Bollinger Bands can be used to trade cryptocurrency successfully because they are an effective signal when it comes to markets being overbought or oversold. The default Bollinger band setting is based on the 20-day moving average and has two standard deviations. The upper band is typically 2 standard deviations above the 20-day moving average and the lower band is set 2 standard deviations below the 20-day moving average. The underlying asset then trades between these two prices with oversold levels reaching the lower band and overbought levels toughing the upper band. The band's width then represents the volatility of the underlying asset.

Fibonacci levels: Fibonacci numbers start with 0 and 1 and then increase exponentially from there by adding the 2 previous numbers together to get the next number in the sequence. As such it starts off with 0, 1, 2, 3, 5 and so on and so forth. The difference between these numbers is known as the Fibonacci ratio which includes .236, .382, .5 and so on and so forth. Finding these ratios in the pairs you are considering allows you to determine naturally occurring entry and exit points.

Price Channels: A price channel is a pair of trend lines that run in parallel to one another. These channels can form so that they are descending, ascending or even horizontal. Price channel lines can often indicate either support or resistance so when the price pass through them and then stays on the other side it is an indicator that a breakout is forming.

The Order Book: As most cryptocurrency exchanges have an order book that you can look at to see a list of all of the transactions that have taken place through the exchange, this order book can be a great indicator as to when a give cryptocurrency is either overbought or oversold. Some exchanges won't make their order book public which is often a sign that they are what is known as a fractal exchange which means they don't keep enough cryptocurrency on hand to handle their responsibilities. As such, if enough people tried to take their funds out of the exchange at once, they would not all be able to and the exchange would fold.

Resistance and Support

Another important tool in analysis is resistance and support levels. When a Cryptocurrency trader identifies these, will get a better sense of the currency's supply and demand levels. A support level is the price where a large number of traders want to buy Cryptocurrency. Traders see Cryptocurrency as being 'oversold' at that point meaning it is sold at a price below its value. As Cryptocurrency starts to approach this price, participants will start buying it and creating a floor.

If the trading price of Cryptocurrency is over for example $10,000 for several days, retreats to this price may cause traders to think the currency is being oversold, and they will begin buying Cryptocurrency causing the price to rise. The price of the Cryptocurrency is irrelevant rather it is the support traders are willing to give it, whether that be $1,000, $10,000 or $100,000.

The opposite to support is resistance. Resistance is a price level where traders are more inclined to sell because they view the security as being 'overbought,' which means that it is overvalued because a lot of traders bought it at high prices.

If the trading price of Cryptocurrency is below $10,000 for several days, a price movement towards $10,000 may cause a lot of traders to sell, which will cause resistance.

Cryptocurrency will often fluctuate between resistance and support, which will create a range. This is what is referred to as 'rangebound trading.' This will create the opportunity for a trader to purchase Cryptocurrency when it is close to the bottom and then sell once it reaches the top.

If the prices of Cryptocurrency were to exit this range, this might cause a lot of trading activity, which will cause volatility, a new trend and in turn new price support and resistance levels.

If the price for Cryptocurrency were to break a level that once was the resistance, this price will end up becoming the new support level. The opposite could happen as well. If the currency's price were to fall below its support level, this level will then become the new resistance.

Considerations

A Cryptocurrency trader can better gauge the market sentiment when they properly leverage technical analysis. They do need to keep a few important variables in mind.

Technical analysis is one of the best approaches since it looks at the volume and price. Also, as Cryptocurrency and Blockchain is currently considered a technical niche it strongly appeals to the tech savvy traders mind.

Risk Management

The next thing you need to look at when you start trading cryptocurrencies is a risk management strategy. No trader is perfect, so there will be a time when a trade becomes a loss. Making sure you have a great risk management system will give you the ability to lose a trade without causing problems or hurting your account. Think about it like this: a trader can have a 50% win rate and make a profit if the expected profit is at least two times as much as a loss. Another trader may have a 75% win rate with a loss that is typically four times as much as what they profit. Here is a formula for the two traders making ten trades:

Trader 1

- $200 average loss

- $400 average gain
- Lost rate of 50%
- Win rate of 50%

[($400)(0.5)]*10 − [($200)(0.5)]*10 = $1000 profit

Trader 2

- $600 average loss
- $150 average gain
- Loss rate of 25%
- Win rate of 75%

[($150)(0.75)]*10 − [($600)(0.25)]*10 = -$375 loss

Trader two might have a better win rate, but they do not make a profit because they did not have a decent risk management strategy. Minimizing how much you lose, is just as important make more winnings through your traders. It is sometimes even easier to limit your losses than it is to increase a win.

Risk and Reward

The best traders will know all of the possible risks and the possible rewards of a trade before they buy in. The goal of trading is to make sure you have a greater reward than a risk. This means the trade has a positive risk to reward ratio. This ratio tells you the amount of money you will risk as compared to the amount of many you believe you will make. An example is if you believe a trade will give you $500 profit, or a possible $100 loss, this ratio is 5:1, making it a favorable trade. On the opposite side of the spectrum, if you will risk $100, but the win is $100, then it is a ratio of 1:1, making it unfavorable.

Calculate your risk to reward ratio every week to ensure you remain profitable. If you see your risk ratio outweigh your reward, then you must analyze your trading strategy and implement a new trading plan.

Scaling Out into Parabolic Moves

Scaling out means that you will only sell a part of your position, typically a quarter or half of the position. Once you have made a little profit you can ride the trend and sell into each candlestick known as selling into parabolic moves. This way a trader can lock in a decent profit as well as the chance of hitting a home run. This will also get rid of some pressure and stress because you know, no matter what happens next, you have already made some profit.

Size Positions Appropriately

The appropriateness of position sizes varies depending on the trader, but a common mistake is having a position that is too large or too small. A large position size will cause you a lot of stress. That is because there is a lot of money on the line and you could end up making a bad decision such as removing yourself too early and not honoring your stops. Always use the two rules stated above of entering small first and increasing your position when your trade has been validated.

Chapter 7: The Future of Cryptocurrencies

Capital markets

Interest in blockchain technology has already been expanding for several years in this sector of the market, with interest in the field doubling yearly for the past three years. This is largely due to the fact that most of the changes to this sector have come in the form of front office technology, leaving the back and middle office to get along in more or less the same way they have for the past few decades. This, in turn, creates situations where an asset is bought or sold instantaneously before then needing to sit around for several days before the paperwork catches up and makes it official.

The Linux foundation is already hard at work on a fix for this problem and is working to bring together blockchain technology and capital market companies through a standardization of a variation of the blockchain technology that will support the existing capital market infrastructure as much as possible. Ideally, this will result in a scenario where a majority of the remaining inefficiency is removed from the system.

As an added bonus, it will also make it possible for those in the field to offer new, and improved ways of providing services to clients while also allowing regulators to determine new and improved ways to optimize settlement and execution times. This will also come along with an increase in transparency that was previously not only unheard of, but impossible. Much of this will come about as a natural result of the way that smart contracts can work to improve efficacy across all levels of the process.

Banking

When it comes to seeing the potential for blockchain banking in the near future, all that is required is a quick look at China who, in 2017, announced that they were in the process of testing their own form of cryptocurrency in transactions between the People's Bank and other commercial alternatives. While many of the details regarding this new cryptocurrency remain unclear, the information that is available indicates that is likely to be rolled out alongside the renminbi, though a firm timetable is still unknown.

This launch will mark a huge step forward towards the legitimacy of blockchain technology and will truly show that cryptocurrency is on its way to being mainstream. It will also likely do wonders for the renminbi as users will be able to purchase it anywhere in the world and have all the benefits of any other traditional fiat currency while also taking advantage of everything that makes cryptocurrency in its current form so useful. It will also help to serve as an interesting proof of concept for national cryptocurrency as a whole because the challenges that Chinese banks will face will have to eventually be overcome by banks everywhere.

China will also see many unique benefits, starting with the fact that their cryptocurrency will allow economists previously unimagined access to the financial data of the country at an extremely granular level. Just what this level of detailed financial data will reveal is still anyone's guess. Even better, the ease of use with which a cryptocurrency can be used will mean that this will mark the first time that millions of Chinese citizens will have an analog for the types of banking services that much of the world takes for granted.

Digital Transactions
With the prevalence of digital transactions that it is regularly used for increasing each day, blockchain technology is likely soon going to reach a point where the core values that it was released to promote are put to the test. Specifically, the US Federal Reserve is in the midst of designing its own cryptocurrency that is internally being referred to as Fedcoin. The Federal Reserve has already held numerous

closed-door meetings with members of the blockchain committee, some of which have been overseen by the chairperson of the Federal reserve herself.

If instituted in the most likely way, Fedcoin will serve to solve the problems that the US government has had with cryptocurrency for the better part of a decade, specifically the fact that it is an obvious outlet for those who are looking to engage in illegal activities online and aren't keen to leave a trace of their activities. This, in turn, means that when it is finally offered to users it will be at the rate of one to one coins to dollars.

Where things start to get complicated, from an ideological level, is that by creating its own cryptocurrency the US government would then have the ability to alter a blockchain once a block has been verified which essentially goes against one of the core tenants of blockchain technology as a whole. Adding this ability to a blockchain will also serve to call its overall legitimacy into question, hurting users' ability to trust it and other similar blockchains as a result, just what the result of this lack of trust will turn out to be remains to be seen.

In general, the Fedcoin blockchain will work the same way as any other blockchain, aside from the major obvious difference.

Additionally, it will remove all anonymity from the blockchain, demolishing another long-held tenant of the technology as well. This will also likely have the effect of putting the use of paper money on a ticking clock as Fedcoin will be easier to track than traditional money as well. The public reception to the rollout of this currency will determine a lot about the way that blockchain technology will be used for digital transactions in the future.

Real Estate

Real estate transactions have a well-earned reputation for being extremely tedious and painstaking to undertake, in large part due to the fact that the industry has experienced very little innovation since the advent of the internet. Blockchain technology is well suited to bringing the industry into the twenty-first century, starting with the listing process. With the right smart contract, as soon as a property hits the listing service blockchain it could be automatically sent to those who are searching for a property that meets its qualifications. Once it becomes commonplace it could practically remove property agents and listing services from the equation entirely.

Instead, buyers, sellers, firms and agents will all be able to interact on one blockchain on an even playing field where anyone will be able to both list or complete real estate transaction around the world without worrying about any third party obfuscating the process. Assuming this platform is built on the Ethereum platform, or another blockchain that promotes application use, then it will also allow for a virtually endless number of apps that will be able to take advantage of the properties that such a platform provides.

As an added bonus, getting rid of the traditional centralized structure will free those on all rungs of the real estate profession to experience with a far greater range of fees than those visible on the market today as they will have far more control of the fees that makes sense on a personal level. The only fees that will be associated with listing on the blockchain will be the ones that come along with verification services and keeping the blockchain up and running. At the same time, it will ensure that buyers have easy access to the latest listings without jumping through too many hoops while also making sure that individual sellers have access to the greatest number of interested buyers possible.

Public services

The myriad of individual organizations that make up the public service sector is enough to make the entire industry a labyrinthine mix of rules and regulations that often makes it difficult for those in charge of providing services to actually go ahead and provide those services. This is largely due to the fact that there is frequently no good way for different departments to share their data. This process is often only exacerbated as department budgets are slashed and the way that services are provided or the services themselves are always being shuffled about.

As blockchain technology continues to become more mainstream, it becomes more and more likely that it will be used to address these types of inefficiencies directly. When properly given the chance, blockchain technology will competently serve as an official registry for numerous different types of things that may require a government license to look at officially. It will also come in handy when it comes to coordinating and streamlining the purchasing process for a wide variety of products, ensuring that each government dollar stretches to the absolute limit. Across the board, it is also sure to improve response times while also reducing the risk of fraud and errors, while at the same time improving productivity and efficiency across virtually all levels of the bureaucracy. As a general rule, wherever governmental inefficiency can be found, a blockchain can be used to stamp it out once and for all.

Industry

Modern business tends to run on the backs of those in a wide variety of administrative positions who do little more than manage various databases and ensure that numbers are recorded properly. Auditing firms, auditors, solicitors, supervisory boards, indeed most of the financial sector exists based on the need for third party verification for some type of transaction or another. As such, the biggest disruption that it will cause in this instance is the removal of a need for most of these services completely.

This improved method of verification is going to create change across a wide variety of industries as distributed ledgers offer up a chance to improve the overall level of trust in each system it is connected to. As every transaction is going to be instantly visible to everyone who is a part of it, it naturally ensures that every contract and even every payment is going to be much more trustworthy than its contemporaries that are made through more traditional systems.

This will then likely result in an extreme shift of power away from those who are in charge of keeping an eye on these transactions, though this will likely not benefit new businesses as much as they might expect. Rather, it will be existing business who will be able to leverage their existing resources in new ways that are going to see the most benefit from this new and improved way of doing business. When done correctly, it will help to ensure that they end up in new, and more profitable, positions than they were previously in.

All told, this will serve to increase the overall rate of adoption for blockchain technology as a whole. This is due to the fact that blockchain technology is inherently social in nature. As such, the more people who use it, the more useful it becomes and so on and so forth until the technology reaches a mass saturation point where more than 50 percent of the population interacts with at least one blockchain a day.

Conclusion

Thank you for making it through to the end of *Cryptocurrency trading: The ultimate guide to trading cryptocurrency for beginners*, let's hope it was informative and able to provide you with all of the tools you need to achieve your goals, whatever it is that they may be. Just because you've finished this book does not mean there is nothing left to learn on the topic, expanding your horizons is the only way to find the mastery you seek.

Do not forget, cryptocurrency is still in its infancy which means that, while this book is useful when it comes to helping you find your footing, you are going to need to make a habit of keeping up with the latest trends if you hope to take advantage of the next big thing. The moment you fall off of the bleeding edge is the moment you run the risk of being uninformed and missing out on a once in a lifetime opportunity.

When it comes to taking advantage of bitcoin for personal profit you will need to decide if you plan to work within the system and promote cryptocurrency directly, or if you are going to trade and invest or even mine. Regardless of which path you choose it is important to have reasonable expectations about how long it is going to take before you start seeing real results. Do not forget, the mass saturation point for cryptocurrency is still an estimated five years away which means any plans you make should be focused on the long-term for the best results. Making a play in the bitcoin market is a marathon, not a sprint, slow and steady wins the race.

Finally, if you found this book useful in any way, a review on Amazon is always appreciated!